Mira Peck

Sour Cherry Tree

To Duncan Douglas
& Judy Douglas,

Best wishes,

Mira Peck 4-16-12

To my ever-patient
David

Contents

Sour Cherry Tree

Contents

I   Poland

Grandpa Ben

He lived in the days before movies
Horse-drawn carts clopped on cobbled streets
Bands of musicians braved heat and snow
Trudging to play in distant towns

He wore a long black beard
Black hat and coat
And a Torah tucked under his arm
As befitted a wizard of his day

The town carousel that he built
whirled with swans and ponies
In white red green and blue

Young boys squeezed into its core
To propel the spokes with bike power
Sending the carousel on its merry twirl
Children's squeals blending in happy dance

The boys were paid not in cash but in the joy
Of riding bikes Ben offered for rent.

The carousel soon burned like the town,
The horses, the children, the swans.

Ben died to the sound of mazurka
Kicked to his knees, dragged by his beard.
He lies buried somewhere unknown
Like the children and the carousel boys

Only we who loved him miss
Honoring his name, marking the place
Where he helped young men
Speed on new machines.

Sour Cherries

From the top of the sour cherry tree
I see wheat fields stretching to the river,
a stork perching on one foot like a ballerina,
a horse-drawn wagon loaded high with hay.

But most of all, I see ripe cherries
all around me like a crimson tutu.
Buckets of cherries if they would only
escape my greedy mouth.

Here at the top they are the sweetest
and somehow the most sour.
I plop one in my mouth, pierce the skin
with my teeth and shudder in ecstasy.

The flavor is tart, bracing, unforgettable,
like a plump raspberry tomato
or a morsel of dark rum chocolate
or a sautéed boletus mushroom.

Sour cherries are to sweet cherries
as red cabernet is to pink zinfandel,
pumpernickel is to Wonder Bread,
sun-ripened tomato is to its poor, cellar-dwelling cousin.

They are worth climbing the tree for.

Sunrays stab my head. I detect the earthy fragrance
of aunt Jasia's dark bread. Soon my mother will call,
Lunch is ready. Where are you? I will swallow another
quick mouthful. I will come down to earth.

I lick my stained hands and pick more berries.
I look for the twins, the ones joined by the stems
that will serve as dangling earrings. If I find
triplets, I'll keep them for luck in my blemished pocket.

Mushroom Picking

Little town of Gunie in primeval forest
Vacation cottage of cousins Jasia, Gieniek,
Bozena, Czesia, Wiesia, Miecia, Marian
orphans who flock here each summer
from children's homes, foster homes, our city home.

Every July at dawn
When newborn mushrooms
poke through the shroud
of pine needles, moss and grass
and no people, deer, squirrels
or other hunters are in sight

Jasia leads the expedition.
She is our expert and guide.
She knows just where to find the lode
How to tell edible morsels
From deadly pretenders.
We follow like chickens a mother hen
searching for bounty along dappled trail.

Suddenly a clan spreads before us:
Boletus boroviki, yellow gaski, buttery maslaki.
Under every clump of grass we find more and more.

Lean sunrays beam through canopy
- Olympic divers stretching for gold.
Fragrances of lilac, damp moss and pine
fill my lungs. I bow down to pick yet another
Boletus, gaska or morelle.
Till my wicker basket is full.

Back at the cottage the cousins
Will sauté these pungent gems
In onion, dill and butter
Until juices flow and the kitchen floods
with the earthy aroma of life.

Mother's Kvas

Standing at attention
Tall glass bottles line
High kitchen shelves
Framing all four walls

Each sealed bottle
Presses chopped rye bread
Sugar and yeast
to ferment, ferment, ferment

Like rebellious teenagers
The liquor foams, bubbles
Rises and at times
Emits a premature pop.

The bursting brown liquid
Splatters the ceiling,
Shelves, and walls
Spreading a pungent aroma.

We thirst for the first bracing sip
Often succumbing too soon
Before the brew reaches
Its full flavor and zest.

To mother's relief
The kvas matures at last
Corks are carefully released
Lest the bottles explode

fall in disarray, shatter on the floor,
stain the white ceiling, white-tile furnace,
bright kilim, flower-print walls
pristine hand-made lace curtains

Mother's ordered life.

Krynki Summer

The one-room farmhouse
Teams with flies
With wood stove, oven, table
And three beds along the walls
>One for uncle and aunt
>One for cousin and his wife
>One for grandma in bed all day
>Coughing into a graying rag.

We choose the hay loft in the distant barn
Skip over mud puddles and tools on the way
Climb the ten-foot ladder
Spread sheets and blankets
On aromatic straw

This is where we'll sleep.
The straw pokes through,
Scratches and digs into our skin
We bounce and laugh

I lay my head on the soft spot
By my mother's breast
My brother under her other arm
We watch stars through uneven planks.

Pigs, chickens, frogs, wolves
All fall silent.
We sigh and slowly
Dissolve into slumber.

Ditta

She is
Eight years old, 1944
Skipping down a Polish city street
Polka-dot dress, red bow
Clasping her ponytail

I am
Eight years old, 1954
She is on a movie screen
Skipping away from me

Dark shadow, German uniform,
Black-gloved hand points
Steel grey gun
At her flying tress

I grip the armrest
Hear the sharp staccato
Scream a silent NO
She is me, I am her

The screen blurs red and grey.
I leave trembling, overcome
Crying inside for Ditta
Who could be me

Father tags my ponytail
Pulls me close
With a sad, vacant smile whispers
"Ditta."

I flinch. What is he thinking!
That I look like his mother?
That I ease his pain?
That I live for the children who died?

I am eight, twenty-eight, forty-eight.
At random moments I am still Ditta.

And she is me.

Music Lessons in Poland

Years ago I ran up those worn steps
Three at a time to fifth floor
My feet ahead of me
Calves flexed and taut

The fat banister ornate and shabby
Walls peeling and ashen
Windowsills dusty and scuffed
Windowpanes cracked from war blasts

I raced to the music streaming
Around hallways to my piano teacher
Stooped and gray fingers wrinkled but plump
From lifetime of daily Chopin mazurkas

After forty years the marble steps
Greet me in renewed glory
I ascend them one at a time admiring
The bronze gleaming banisters

Fresh mauve walls
Windowsills mahogany sheen
And as I look up my eyes
lock on a new surprise:

Ceiling fresco then faint under film
Of age and neglect now majestic
Fluid bodies in flowing robes
White clouds and pink magnolias

A maiden strumming a harp
A cherub blowing a trumpet
Making music like my adolescent self
Fingers dancing pirouettes and minuets

Behind me my children scale
The steps in youthful joy
Perceiving ever so slightly if at all
How I was once like them

How I wish for them what I had
Only without squalor shattered windows
And the wistful memories
Of derailed promise

Katyn Forest 1940

A linguistic oddity:
Kat (kaht) n. [Polish]
= Executioner

Now the world knows that
twenty thousand Polish officers
were shot in the Katyn Forest
I must ask.

Why is the site solemnized
with groves of crosses,
statues of Jesus, Mother Mary,
flight-winged angels,
supplicating saints?

Michal Midler, a dentist, a Jew
Lies among the dead
Unavenged,
Unmarked,
Unhonored.

Yet he too wore the uniform
Of a Polish lieutenant.
And his white-eagle cap
Fell into the grave with the others.

His cells mingle with those of
freethinkers, Muslims, Buddhists,
Baptists, Hindus and Jews.

Killed once,
Forgotten twice.

II   Australia

Ayers Rock Tent Dwellers

The desert seems dead until
you rouse from slumber, not alone,
but sharing your face with strangers
creeping on your cheek.

You still your breath and ponder:
A brood of corpulent spiders?
A swarm of dizzy maggots?
A horde of insane bedbugs?

You do not wish to become a hunk
of kangaroo steak or an emu sandwich,
So you channel fear to your brain's
right lobe and implore it to save you.

In a clap of thunder you snap your parka
up and across, hold the wriggling booty
at arm's length, impale it
with a flashlight…

Later you may chitchat about adventure
but no palaver can mock your encounter
with a ten-inch scorpion, its fearsome tail
poised to strike the next prey.

The venom will kill a katydid, a frog, a gecko,
but not you. And you know the crook of its tail
connects the chain: ant to spider to scorpion
to pink-crested galah to emu to eagle.

So you slowly rise,
crawl through the tent's open flap,
and set it free.

The Vaulting Horse

On a blisteringly hot Australian January day in 1963, I stand in line of high school students. It is my first gym class in a new school and a new country. In its vastness, polished hardwood floor and exercise equipment along the tall walls, the gym resembles the Polish one I had left three months earlier. In its center, atop green rubber mats, waits a vaulting horse, a leather-padded bench on four wooden legs that reaches up to the waists of the two teachers poised at each end.

The familiarity comforts me: I have made many jumps over just such a contraption during my recent childhood in Poland, and I'm eager to resume my athletic life. I hear the instructions in the foreign tongue, and then watch each girl ahead of me, in turn, trot to the bench, place her hands on its surface, and bounce to the top onto her knees. The teachers grip her forearms and help her slide down.

It's my turn. I inhale, sprint, jump high, clear the top and nail the landing on the other side. I'm happy I haven't lost the skill during the idle months of immigration. I stretch my arms for the dismount, straighten legs and back, and run to the end of the line, ready for my next turn.

Then silence. My classmates' puzzled faces signal that something is wrong. I gaze towards the teachers and see them both standing still, glaring at me. One of them says something in the noodle-chewing English that took me months to comprehend. An earlier Polish arrival translates the message: "What you did is very dangerous for girls. Next time watch the others and do as they do."

But I've done this many times! I want to say. I am bewildered. What's gender got to do with it? Maybe they think it's a fluke that I jumped over. If I do it again, surely they'll change their minds.

At my next turn, I begin the sprint when a loud voice calls, "Stop!"

Too late. I'm already clearing the bench and landing. The teacher extends his arm to block me from returning to the line. I look up at him as he barks unintelligible commands at me and summons the interpreter.

"You'll be suspended from school if you don't follow the rules," she translates.

My throat constricts. I want to bolt, fly back to Poland where I belong, where I can run and jump and plan to be my country's president.

But I'm stuck. I'm only sixteen and ten thousand miles away. Being a functional mute makes me feel helpless many times, and this is one of them.

In time I learn to follow the prescribed feminine routine. I fall into the comfort of blending in, and slowly forget the exhilaration of the fast run, the high jump, the feeling of accomplishment on the other side.

My next clear memory is of standing in the gym some weeks later, mentally disengaged, moving forward in a line of girls, then lethargically trotting up to the vaulting horse without momentum and finding it large, looming, so tall that I can barely muster the courage to hoist myself all the way up to its precarious surface. Once on top, I grip the hands of the two teachers who ease me back down.

But once there was a time when I was able to jump over this monster. Wasn't there?

Tears press under my eyelids. I squash them down, all the way down to my aching belly where they will hibernate with my spirit.

The Melbourne Queen Victoria Market

Sunday sunrise the rambling tram carries me
downtown. My eyelids droop from a late library night.
When the ocean's glitter stows behind low brick houses
I jerk my head and read street signs:
Elizabeth, Queen, William, King,

At last the majestic Victoria Parade. The engine
groans to a stop. I step down, pass deli cases,
count ten varieties of olives, six shades of white
feta cheese, countless shelves of breads, graceful,
squat, long and round. So enticing, but no time now.

I stride along a bustling alley of papaws, plums, peaches.
A left turn and the noise dulls in the new world
of kangaroo fur slippers, cozy sheepskin rugs, Aboriginal
Dreamland tee-shirts waving in warm breeze,
Frilled-neck pewter lizards gazing through opal eyes.

Mr. Bergman nods and smiles. I'm a two-year veteran.
 I know what to do. I open each cardboard box,
carefully place men's V-necks along the left edge,
button-down cardigans flanking right, cascading
from small to large to extra large in progression
of a well-fed life. In the center, baby pyjamas in blue, pink,
and yellow for parents eager to thwart gender coding.

One last section remains. I shimmy my aching back,
stretch my arms up like a swimmer, then reach
for the showpiece tempting browsers to turn the corner:
a hand-embroidered angora jacket. I suspend it
high on the solid wrought iron I-beam.

Scanning the disciplined formation of throne pretenders,
I glance at the tomato-cheeked women unloading potatoes
from trucks, arranging portly cabbages and eggplants,
dainty fiddleheads and pearl onions, plump red radishes
and burly white parsnips still clinging to black loam.

In hard-earned accents they shout "Two for a quid, senora,
is beaut!" and offer the bounty with earthy hands.
Behind the makeshift counters their children, like me,
with clean fingers and polite smiles, collect the cash,
return correct change, say *ta*, madam, act as if they belong.

Gates of Sand

*John Howard, 1947-1977, loving
husband to Ann, devoted father of
Anthony, 5 and Michael, 3; beloved
son of Melinda and Geoffrey; only
brother of Helen. Passed away during
the Melbourne to Hobart race. Deeply
missed by family and friends.*

Backstory

How he stayed on deck at night while his father and uncle
rested below. How a rogue wave pummeled the vessel, nearly
tipping it over. How his father scrambled up swaying steps,
shouting John, John, above the storm's roar. How the crew,
now reduced to two, circled the turbulent dark water
illuminated only by lightning, spotlights and flashlights, until
dawn.

How they hoped his strong arms carried him back to the shore.
How they looked for his face among the waiting throng. How
their eyes followed the jetty and sank to the ocean's floor. How
they fought imagining him torn by hammerhead sharks and
sharp coral.

How his mother lay prostrate in sorrow. How his wife waited
years before marrying again. How his sons grew up calling
another man daddy. How a friend he had plucked out of
isolation still can't believe he is gone.

Halina

She was nine years and eighty pounds
When the Nazi officer stormed her Poznan home
Barking, raus, raus, while his men sang
German army songs and carried away her antique bed,
Piano, postage stamp collection and favorite doll.

At ten years and eighty pounds
She was locked within ghetto walls
In an airless dungeon for sixteen hours each day
Breathing leather tanning fumes
Her skin one spectral sore.

At twelve years and eighty pounds
Cattle train rumbled beneath her feet
For three days to the Birkenau swamp
Schnell, schnell, the armed soldiers urged
Shaving heads, searching mouths and fingers for gold.

At thirteen and eighty pounds
A windowless convoy delivered her to the Baltic Sea
She watched the Camp Stutthof commandant play
Beyond barbed wire with his toddler and pet dog
then publically hang young Russian boys.

She was fourteen and eighty pounds
When the guard caught her speaking
And beat her with a whistling oak branch
Until the sand beneath her turned red.

Take a look at her smiling face
Walk through her garden of golden wattles
Hear the warbling of crimson rosellas.

Life after Death

I had to see you
Before the final burial
Begged till they bent the rules
Wheeled you in, frozen
Wrapped in plain white cloth.

The shomer carefully
Untied the wrinkled cotton
Formed over familiar hollows
And ridges of your shape ...

He said – no kissing
Your father was washed clean
I nodded, thistle-throated
Moved dreamwalking closer
To your unveiling face

You looked barely dozing
Almost ready to wink
Only very pale
Under dark gray stubble

My finger traced the outline of
Your black bushy brows
Small brown birthmark
Smooth cheekbone skin
Strong trademark nose

Cold, hard,
You and not you
Now I believed you
Dead

I walked around you
Wanting to see more
Face   ears   mouth
Funny nostril hairs

One last look
                    Air kiss
                                I love you

All quiet, finished, still
But the dark stubble grows
Strong, tough, defiant
Persistent

Like me
Your life after death.

The Pier on Port Phillip Bay

The sun probably shone, but I don't remember.
The ocean probably glittered. Australian winter,
mild, breezy day. We strolled from Elwood to
Port Phillip Bay, past dog walkers, bikers, runners.
I remember my father's contented smile and my pleasure
that our eyes, mouths, brows, looked the same.
We probably talked about my new house in America.
He worried how expensive it was. He probably said,
"If you need to fix it, build new cabinets, a new sunroom,
let me know." I probably asked about his house renovation job,
he probably said everything cost more now but he had friends,
German glazier, Italian bricklayer, Czech plumber.
We ambled side by side toward the jetty framed in blue
and the city skyline. I dueled with thoughts that this might be
my last time to see him, or his last time to see me.
I wished them away. Our promenade should flow
without sorrow. The round café trimming the pier intruded
like a period marking the end of a sentence. No, I told myself
over cappuccino and warm biscuits, it's only a comma.
Five years sailed by. I trudged down the same crunching sand.
It was May again, mild, breezy day. My eyes burned, throat
ached. The fresh espresso soothed me, ocean wind played in
my hair. Upon each return I retrace our steps down the bay.

Ode to Tiffany

You, twenty pound Schipperkee,
keep my mother alive.
You bark ferociously at the mastiff
guarding his gate next door
and cow him into silence.

You are her protector, her secretary.
You squeak a stubborn staccato
urging her from the garden
when the phone rings.

How do you know it's her child
calling from afar?

Not even her son or daughter
receive your exuberant welcome.
You whimper and sniff by the door
till she comes home.

Keen eyes
Black hair
Stubby legs
No tail

Bred to herd sheep onto
Belgian canal decks
and nip at shins of horses
pulling the boats along,

you are loyal and fierce,
the guardrail she needs
to keep her safe and steady
on the rocking ferry.

The Contortionist

Father said feel as I feel
        She wrapped left thigh twice around her neck

Mother said be good so people won't talk
        She twisted right calf thrice across her hips

Brother said be a good sister, read my mind
        She threaded left arm between her legs and torso

Teacher said you're a girl, don't be so smart
        She folded right arm backwards hand over her eyes

Husband said I am listening isn't that piliated woodpecker
        in the Metasequoia Glyptostroboidis beautiful?
        She twirled her brain around the cortex, found
        virtual love

If one stops training a bonsai tree
Will it slowly unfurl its branches
Release its hidden center
Stretch like a giant cedar?

III America

Hal Comes Through

Hal Brody's Process Engineering department had been in existence for two years, before I joined in 1974 as the sixth engineer. Hal had been brought over to the century-old Putnam production plant by the Philadelphia corporate headquarters, to introduce state-of-the-art technology. Many of the site's managers viewed him and his sharpshooters as interlopers.

In selecting his team Hal paid careful attention to each member's ability to get along with people. Without diplomacy our clever designs would be for naught, as the manufacturing supervisors could sabotage our efforts. Within our group we also got along well. We worked long hours, often supervising critical production steps on night shift, but at weekly staff meetings or lunchtime bridge games in Hal's office, we relaxed and bantered with each other. For the first time, I worked in my chosen field and felt accepted by my colleagues.

The Putnam site was laid out like a small city, with production buildings, laboratories and warehouses lining each side of the main street. My first project required laboratory tests of a modernized process before scaling it up to full production volume. One morning while on my way to the lab, I heard a loud wolf-whistle. Turning my head I saw two men dressed in overalls waving in my direction.

"Hey, mama, looking good."

"Hey, babe, what's your name?"

I halted. As the first woman engineer I had expected some adjustment, but, no matter how alone and aberrant I might feel I would not be demeaned.

I turned to face them, my safety goggles, steel-toed boots and managerial white helmet my only protection. One heckler was young and slender, the other, older and squat. Both wore helmets identical to mine, except yellow to indicate hourly maintenance workers.

"Please don't be rude," I said. "I work here just like you."

They looked at each other and laughed. "Lady, don't be so uptight," the older one chided. "You a women's libber or somethin'?"

"You're the new girl that Brody hired to keep us in line, right?" The younger one gibed.

His jeering unnerved me like a dog's bared teeth. "Yes, I'm the new engineer."

"But what's a pretty girl like you doing in a man's job?" the squat one taunted.

Underneath my astronaut getup, he couldn't see my face. Even my breasts were covered with a zippered jacket. I was a generic woman, and that was enough.

Pressure built in my chest. I was new, foreign, vulnerable. If I let myself express anger, I might lose control, scream, and end up being accused of hysteria. I turned and hurried towards the lab, trailed by whistles and catcalls. I wadded my shaking hands into tight fists in my pockets, where nobody could see, and marched on, eyes welling with tears.

A couple of hours later, I scanned the road that led back to my office and saw, to my relief, that the men had gone. But for the next few mornings, their taunts continued.

What to do? I wanted to blend in, but accepting humiliation didn't feel right. My life would be miserable. And what a precedent for other women!

At home that evening, I turned to Wayne for advice. "Do you think I'm over-reacting? Should I let it go and hope these men will stop?"

Wayne thought for a moment as he cut cucumber and tomatoes into his daily salad bowl. "That's one way to handle it. But I don't think you'd be happy. Why don't you talk to Hal? He seems like an enlightened man. See what he says."

Thus emboldened, the next morning I popped into Hal's office.

"May I see you for a moment?"

"Sure, come in." Hal's blue eyes had their usual twinkle, making me feel welcome. I sat down across from him.

Lacking John Wayne's physique, Hal would poke fun at himself about being a little Napoleon, but, like the emperor, he exuded unflappable confidence. Still muscular, as he must have been to win the college wrestling trophies on his shelf, he would challenge men in our group to arm-wrestle. Invariably, he won. He was a winner in life, too, and his charisma was the main reason I had accepted my position.

"What's up? How's the job coming along?"

I shifted in the chair. Hal had promised to support me, but this was the first time I came to him with a complaint.

"It's fine, the job is fine," I said. "I like my project. Phase separation technology is just what I wanted to do. The only thing is –"

He prodded amiably, "Is something bothering you?"

"Yes," I said, then laid it out in a single sentence afraid to lose my resolve. "When I walk to the lab, these men outside the maintenance building whistle and make tasteless remarks."

"What do they say? I'd like to know so I can deal with it."

"Oh, you know, they call me babe and mama and ask what's a *girl* doing in a man's job."

A little smile played on his lips, "So, did you tell them to go back to their cave?"

Startled and reassured by his empathy, I said, "Not quite. I tried to be polite and told them to please not be rude."

Hal shook his head. "You're too much of a lady. You should tell those guys to go pound sand. But I'm glad you told me. I don't want anyone treating my engineers with disrespect." He buzzed his secretary. "Linda, get me Dr. Winston on the line, please."

A man's voice came over on the speaker phone. "Hey there, Hal, how are things?"

"Not bad, Wally. When are you coming over for a game of bridge?"

"I've a meeting today, but how about tomorrow??"

"Come over at noon. We'll buy you coffee, and I'll introduce you to a new engineer we just hired. She'll be working on the solvent recovery project with your team."

"That's great. The state's breathing down our necks."

"Alina Sherwin is here with me." Hal motioned me to the speaker phone.

"Hello, Wally, this is Alina. I look forward to working with you."

"Welcome on board. How's your bridge game?"

"Pretty rough," I laughed. "But Hal's a good teacher. Soon I might even trump him."

"Let's take him on together. You want to partner with me?"

Hal leaned towards the phone. "Sure, she could, but you gotta help us first. Some of your guys need to learn how to treat women at work. I want you to talk to them."

"Which guys?" Wally pushed back. "What did they do?"

Hal raised his eyes to me. "It's not important who they are; they all must act professionally. They shouldn't whistle or make inappropriate remarks, like calling a colleague 'babe' and 'mama.' This is not a corner pub."

Wally was silent for a moment. This was probably a new concern for him. "They were just being friendly. Come on, it's no big deal."

"Wally, you're wrong. It *is* a big deal. I don't want my engineers to be jeered. You gotta talk to your guys. Soon. She's going to the lab this morning. If they don't act with respect, then she won't be happy. And I won't be happy. We need to work together on this."

"Well, okay. I'll talk to them. Alina, if they bother you again, you call me, all right?"

"Thanks, I will."

"I'll see you tomorrow. Hal, you better watch it or Alina and I will beat your pants off."

"Not a chance. She'll be handicapped by you. G'bye." Hal hung up and gave me a conspiratorial grin. "He's a good man, but a bit old-fashioned. Let me know how it goes today."

The next day Wally and I lost the bridge game to Hal and Rich by a narrow margin. But I was glad we met him in a social setting. Wally had a soft, jowly face, tousled ash-brown hair, and a piercing gaze. I suspected that not much got by him.

He was in a tough situation, too. The production site, originally owned by a giant German conglomerate, was recently acquired by a US corporation. The ten or so German PhD chemists who had remained, perpetuated outdated technology, prompting the new management to hire local scientists and engineers. Wally was the first, and so far the only, chemist with a doctorate from an American university. He came on board around the same time as Hal, and could be a natural ally for our group. I was beginning to recognize office politics and getting an inkling of Hal's mastery.

On the oak tree outside my office window, a bird in a nest was feeding a worm to its chicks. It was early April and spring was poised to punch winter for a knockout. I reclined in my chair and scanned the news in the Lancaster daily. President Nixon's Watergate scandal was escalating; the Symbionese Liberation Army still held Patricia Hearst captive; and OPEC ended the oil embargo it imposed in 1973 during the Yom Kippur War.

The business section featured a megastore opening and… was that my name? Below the bolded heading, Employment News, I read a paragraph about my new position at Salinger Colors, Inc. Why were they writing about me of all people? Did Hal have something to do with it? With the article in hand, I knocked on Hal's open door. He was on the phone but pointed to the chair across from him.

"You bet," he said. "We'll put our best people on it. G'bye." He hung up and told me, "That was my boss. Things are heating up on those solvent wastes. We'll have to put a priority on it. What you got?"

"I saw my name in today's paper," I said, placing the page on his desk. "I haven't done anything special, so why are they writing about me?"

"Oh, that. It's normal practice for companies to report new hires, and some of them get printed. It's a way for Salinger to publicize its modernization campaigns."

"So I'm promoting the company's good name just by being on its payroll, huh?"

Hal gave me a wry smile. "That's right. But don't worry. Pretty soon you'll be making good on the promise. Why don't you close the door and let's talk."

I did as he asked, and sat down.

Hal continued. "We have a small group and a hell of a lot of work to do. Hundreds of 55-gallon drums with spent solvents are stacked up on the site - many are rusting and possibly leaking. Several storage tanks are full of the stuff. In most cases we don't know what's in them; it could be any mix of the twenty different chemicals used over decades. It's an environmental nightmare."

"Not only that," I added, "but with the oil shortage, some solvents could be reused, or reclaimed and sold. Or burned as fuel."

"You've got the right idea. So how would you like to manage solvent recovery for this production site?"

"The whole site? That's a big responsibility for a newbie."

"You're a good manager and you won't have to do it alone. I want you to organize a team of specialists from different departments, develop an action plan, and run with it."

"Would I be responsible for proposing a long-term solution for solvent recycling, including equipment design?"

"That makes sense. We've got to get rid of the waste, and bring this plant into modern age."

I couldn't believe my luck: after less that two months with the company, I'd be spearheading a major project.

"Hal, I'm flattered. Of course I'll take it on."

He tapped the desk with his pen and sat back. "How are you getting along with those maintenance technicians? They still bothering you?"

"Not since your talk to Wally. In fact, both helped me set up equipment for the trial production batch and they behaved like perfect gentlemen."

"Most of them are good guys. They will treat you with respect if you show them you know your stuff." He leaned forward and met my eyes. "Have you considered graduate school?"

"I'd like to get an MBA. An American degree would obviate questions about my foreign degree. The classes would have to be in the evening or on weekends, and then there's the cost…"

"The company would pay tuition."

"Really?"

"Sure. We want to invest in good employees. Get Personnel to help you explore MBA programs and I'll sign off on it."

I suppressed the urge to throw my arms around him and cry. Instead, I replied calmly, "I'll get on it right away."

Medieval Warrior

Where does fear reside
In a warrior's suit of armor?
Is it between the heavy metal helmet
And the chain mail on the chest?

It could be in other parts
But the vulnerable spot on the neck
Is an easy target for a strong enemy
Outfitted with a sharp lance.

Or does fear spread over the belly
There, where a precise weapon
Can slide in sideways
And cut through liver or guts?

One can admire the strength needed
To put this iron cage on one's body
To lift one's burdened arms
And swing…

Or one can tremble in immobilizing terror
Of being crushed, impaled and left for dead.

All of the glories
        Of mortal battle.

The Corporate Seal

In the corporate world
I stifle my feelings till
I don't know what matters
And what to let go.

I shift my priorities
Away from the impossible
Rearrange my life wiser
Revise my dreams.

I dive into learning
In hopeful frenzy
To drown anger
      dilute energy
           hold on to ME…

Like a dancing seal
I swim wall to wall
Jump through hoops
Bark in six tongues
Twirl a silver
Ball on my nose

I flip for fresh tuna
My promised reward
But get only chum
      and jump hoops
      and balls

I quietly teach
Their chosen ones
Who feed on my tuna
And blossom and grow
And bask in the light
Of my silver ball

I watch amazed
Almost beyond anger
As they break faith
With me and my sisters
From whom I am
Estranged…

We all watch
Alone
Well trained
In silence.

The Corporate Master

I am facing the corporate master
Charming and smooth
Who nimbly restates my words
And builds a scenario
In which he will shine.

I am part brick, part bricklayer
Attempting to pave a path
Through navigable terrain
For me and those who will follow.

If this is the only landscape that exists
I the bricklayer could lay a smooth road
To the wizard's castle
Or I the brick could hurl down the slope
And shatter to pieces.

With predator's blue eyes
He searches for my artery
He roars you're inflexible
You must learn to bend

The master hits bull's eye – but he
Rigidly cuts heads, twists messages,
Reveals only his truth
(Or is he focused, fervent and wise?)

He tells me to trade small losses
For big victories.
In his world this is right.
Those who don't count – cower before him.
Those who matter - propel him to the top.

The path splits into many
And predators' piercing eyes
Lurk behind every boulder
While I, appalled and hopeful,
Learn how it's done.

Effigy

Her voice carried high
Above the audience
She was Virginia Woolf
And everyone was afraid

She bandied about the stage
Boom and vigor
Eyes burning, words blasting
Fingers, arms

This could have been Broadway
But it was Albany
Her other life tossed her
From one state to the next

As she followed the husband she loved
Nurtured two daughters
Pouring her glamour
Into them

By midlife she returned
To the big stage
As a servant, a hag, a whore
Never again Virginia Woolf

Her hands, restless, longed to feel
So she sculpted lustful pears,
Moon Ladies, phantoms hidden
In veined marble from Italy

When art lovers gathered
She played star again
Her self unveiled
To an applauding world.

Alice

Tribute to
Dr. Alice Lazzarini,
Pioneering Geneticist,
Author of Both Sides Now,
a memoir of her journey from
Parkinson's researcher to patient

Store clerks and passersby would stop and marvel at her big blue
eyes   Adorable baby, what a lovely baby, Gerber Baby   She
passed on her genes to her offspring who grew into Gerber Babies
and passed on their genes to more Gerber Babies   Enchanting
babies as blue eyed as she was then   Now one eye is grey and
doesn't open as much as the other and when she smiles the
photographer tells her not to arch her right brow   I'm not arching
she says but the camera doesn't lie   Her eyelids droop   hips tilt
feet totter   Her hand trembles as she lifts sushi to her quivering lips
 She's in a race to find a cure and write down her story   Already
her work day must end at sundown   As her quakes escalate she
 watches for tremors in her children and their children

Porcupine Peg

Peggy hates
Rages at the world
Talks loudly at dinner
Shouts in restaurants

Peggy fears
Stepping out in the morning
Bad people on the bus might
Yell, hurt, kill

Peggy lived
In a house of hard people
Whose love was buried
In screams, raised fists, angry faces

Peggy remembers
Saucers flying low without warning
Shattering on flower print walls
Potted ferns whooshing by
Spilling dirt and roots
Joining the brown pottery shards
On her parents' vinyl floor

Peggy loves
The baby in her womb
The man who stays around
And holds her after a row

Peggy fights
Quick, loud and sharp
She scares and awes
To save herself from harm

Peggy admires
My restraint and good manners
But she teaches me to defy people
Who are fierce like her

She draws me
To her thorny self.
I love her as I hate her
And we both grow.

A Place in the Universe

I reached an impossible height
by all rights I deserved but always
expectation of failure and loss
lurked just under my skin.

Ancient voices whispered:
enjoy it while it lasts,
after you're happy you'll cry,
who are you to aspire high?
Watch out.

To bolster me and themselves
my parents said, you make us proud.
Our daughter can do anything,
go anywhere, be anyone.

As I clawed to get what others
like me were denied I saw:

My father's ethnic face,
an immigrant amid gloss, eyes
flittering from my assistant to me,
incredulous at my success;

My mother's smiling bravado,
defying the world to stop her
from getting respect, a job, a house,
a peaceful life.

I believed what I saw
and dismissed what I heard.
After forty years, four tongues,
four countries, four degrees
that ominous voice still whispers:

Watch out.

IV   A Place in the Universe

Nangka

Frail old man buckles under
the weight of spiky fruit,
massive, curved and plump,
a giant's kidney.

Other merchants mock him,
their teeth stained red
by the beetlenut they all chew.
He laughs indulgently,

hefts the beast on top
of his barren fruit stand, lays it
next to three mangoes and two papayas,
motions the white couple to watch.

He flicks a long, rusty knife,
offers her a slice of saffron flesh
and him an apricot-hued ball clinging
to a pit pried from its juicy depths.

They have already braved
Fresh crocodile stew
and coconut beetle larvae
slathered in red burning spice.

The pungent, cloying odor repels
and draws them.
They are, after all, hitchhikers
on a long discovery voyage.

Nangka, the old man says
then breaks into rapid chatter,
bony hands and arms flying,
gesturing eat, eat, mmm…

And they do.

Galia's Quest

<u>At age six</u>
"Mommy, did I come out of your tummy?" Galia asks from the back seat as we drive to the shore.

"Honey, everyone comes out of a mommy's tummy."

"But did I come out of your tummy?"

Here, my son, Oleg, who's also six and was adopted at the same time, chimes in matter-of-factly, "You came out of a tummy, but not out of mommy's tummy."

Galia persists. "Mommy, did I come out of *your* tummy?"

I wait until we park the car, then slide out of my seat, open her door, and hold her slender hand. "Not my tummy," I capitulate.

"Why not?" She stares me down with her intense, dark eyes.

"Because I wasn't lucky enough to have you," I say, unable to think of anything better at the moment. I'm trying to shield her from agonizing over the reasons that her birth mother and father gave her up. She's still such a little girl, still plays with dolls and likes to pretend she's a baby suckling at my breast. I want her to be a child and not think grownup thoughts.

But she's on to me. "That's not an answer." Her lower lip quivers. I try to embrace her, but she wriggles away, leaving me with my arms empty.

Well, I think, at least I didn't lie. I'll try to have a better answer next time.

My husband and I never hide the fact that we adopted her; that we brought her happily home with us to America from Russia. She likes to hear the stories about our visit to her orphanage in Volgograd; about the dog Tzina she played with, the mega-scale memorial to her heroic kin who sacrificed their lives to stop the Nazi invaders.

I'm gratified when, after blowing out five birthday candles, she says, in Russian: "Mama, when I was still in the orphanage, you sent me a heart necklace and a heart ring from America, for my fourth birthday, remember?"

But these encouraging insights are rare. More often, she seems to forget, or perhaps refuses to accept, what we already told her.

During a visit to my in-laws' farm, she giggles while watching piglets suckle their mother. Suddenly, she frowns and looks at me sternly. "Mama, did you adopt me?"

"Yes, darling, we did," I reply with a smile.

She yanks her hand out of mine. "Then you are not my mother."

My husband lifts her and cradles her in his arms. "She is your mother," he says softly. "There can be two kinds of mothers: the birth mother and the mother who raises you."

She slumps against his shoulder, scrunches her face in utter sorrow, and cries.

I want to hold her close and cry with her. When our tears are spent, I want to see her laugh and play. I hope fervently that we can pacify her, just by steady patience and love.

But it's a hard road. She likes to get gifts often, as if that were proof of her value. We do what we can to show her how precious she is to us, but we cannot fix her past.

At age ten

Galia works on an assignment for her Sunday school. The topic is "Your Ancestors." She asks me to help her answer questions such as: where are your ancestors from? When did they leave their country? During what period of history? Why did they leave? Do you observe any traditions from that homeland? Galia writes that her mother emigrated from Poland to Australia for a better life, then came to the USA with her American husband, and that Galia herself came here after being adopted. I'm thrilled that she feels this connection to me, yet can't help worrying about the confusion such questions may cause her.

Once Galia completes her assignment, I help her get ready for a play date with her twelve-year old friend, Debbie.

"Mommy," she says, "why doesn't Debbie live with her mommy and daddy?"

Debbie has been put in a children's shelter because her biological father abused her. In an effort to find an adoptive family, Debbie's counselors have placed an ad in our community paper, citing her "abuse and many losses."

Trying to spare Galia from grieving for her friend's tragedy, I answer neutrally, "Sometimes children are better off living with other people."

"Could we adopt her?" Galia asks.

"That's such a sweet idea. Let's think about it."

The dilemma resolves itself. After her play date, Galia tells me that Debbie is moving far away.

That evening Galia is taking a bath. As I sponge her feet, she says in her melodic voice:

"I'm glad I was adopted. I'm glad I have a good family and a nice home."

"That's wonderful, darling. And I'm glad you're my daughter."

"Really? But I'm bad and I say bad things."

"No, you're a wonderful girl. You're a child, and you're still learning. We're all learning. We all do and say things we regret. But you have a good heart, and you'll figure it out. You're my sweet girl forever."

Two days later she's in bed, ready for her goodnight back-scratch. When I bend down, she loops her long, slender arms around my neck, tickles my cheek with her eyelashes and asks me to do the same. We laugh.

She reaches under her pillow and pulls out an issue of the National Geographic. "My family," she says, pointing to the cover.

It's a color photograph of Moscow's Kremlin. I wince.

"My family," she repeats, pointing again. "In Russia."

"Yes," I say. "Your birth family is in Russia. But you are luckier than most little girls, because you have two families. And we love you very much. Want to flip over on your tummy?"

I say this lightly, bit I'm momentarily fatigued by the Sisyphean task of pushing a boulder up a mountain, only to watch it roll back down again.

<u>At age eleven</u>

Galia and Oleg attend CampQuest in Ohio, their first sleep-away camp. Oleg immediately joins the children throwing Frisbee, but Galia clings to my husband and me. An amiable student-volunteer succeeds in coaxing her to have some ice cream by the pool. Seeing her giggle and splash her feet in the water eases our discomfort at leaving her for a week. After most of the parents are gone, we slip away and drive home. From the camp's literature, we know that many enjoyable activities are planned: swimming, canoeing, hiking, roasting marshmallows on campfire. The children will also continue the tradition of looking for the invisible unicorn. For the past ten years, the search failed, leaving the elusive creature for next year's campers to find.

When my husband and I arrive the following Saturday, both children jump into our outstretched arms. They squeal excitedly, about the first meteor shower they ever saw, about the swimming races and new friends.

"Did you find the unicorn?" I ask.

Galia takes my hand, looks in my face and whispers: "I didn't find the unicorn, but I found two angels."

"How did they look?" I express my usual skepticism.

"The boy was tall and blond, the girl shorter and dark-haired." Her description matches her Dad and me. "They were my angels because they adopted me so I could have a home."

At age twelve

After visiting the exploitative Build-a-Bear emporium that inexplicably thrills my kids, Galia and I stop at an Ecuadorian store. It's stocked with turquoise pendants, dream catchers as big as dinner plates, sheepskin rugs designed with llamas and bison, and earth-hued, coarse wool sweaters. Galia tries on a jacket, then a second, then a third one that feels soft and looks 'cool' on her.

I hear her say, "I like the blue one."

"This one?" I pick up the blue jacket that has an image of wolves howling at the moon.

"No," she points to the one in grey, with a bison. "I said I like the bull one."

We laugh. She inspects herself in the mirror, tries on the hood, stuffs her hands in the pockets. She looks lovely, and obviously enjoys the thought of wearing this unusual, cozy garment. I buy it, a gift for her birthday.

Back in the car, Galia declares: "I'm lucky you adopted me. If you didn't take me, I'd probably still be at the orphanage."

I wait a moment to bask in her new realization, then say, "We're lucky too. We have a daughter who's smart, thoughtful, likes to read books." I glance at her with a grin. "And who asks good questions."

She raises her eyebrows in surprise. "I do?"

"Yes, you clever girl. You bring us a lot of joy."

Several weeks later, another incident gives me hope of a breakthrough. When I stop by after Galia's class, her teacher walks alongside me to the lunchroom and whispers: "It was so sweet. Today we talked about our heroes. The other children said they admire Lance

Armstrong and Golda Meir and Martin Luther King. But Galia said that the person she admires most is her mom."

"Really?" I say, surprised and elated. "That is wonderful."

When Galia is older and asks about her biological family, I'll tell her all that I know. If she chooses to look for her birth parents, I hope her search will be more fulfilling than her hunt for the unicorn. If she finds them, I wish her acceptance and joy, not rejection and pain. For her sake, I want them to be good people.

And for my sake, I want her to be a good person, able to feel love for both mothers.

My Son

My son is fireworks over dark horizon
brilliant reds and yellows illuminating
roof tops and treetops
in precise outlines

His laughter crackles and explodes
in stories
lyrics
punchlines

My son is Nintendo dragons
extreme bicycle rides
go-kart crashes
black and blue medals on his arms

His hair tumbles in unruly waterfalls
eyebrows black and assertive
exclamation marks
poised to rise

He is Green Day
Slipknot
The Beatles
Stevie Wonder's Sunshine of My Life

An iPod with a thousand tunes
is my son

Late Motherhood

A tall man in shorts ambles up the path
Slightly leaning left
To hold the hand of the little boy
In sandals and a polo shirt like daddy's

Behind them a brunette
In a strapless dress leans sideways
To hold the hand of the little girl
Who skips and wriggles beside her

Now that I am a mother I can tell
The boy is about 5, the girl about 3
I now notice their cute outfits
As future fashions for my own kids

Now I know the pleasure of riffling
Through racks of children's clothes
Tiny swimsuits with flowers or supermen
Tiny short-sets with giraffes and lions
Tiny striped baseball uniforms
Tiny frilly dresses and leggings

As I watch the family outside my office window
I am struck that a year ago
I would've looked at them wistfully
Felt the pain somewhere in my body
Told myself "just as well"

A year ago I would have resigned
To my bio clock,
My sadness that I missed this in life
My future decades to fill

Now this scene touches my center
I have everything I want
As a woman, a person, a thinker
As a worker, a lover, a mother

My children run to me screaming "Mama!!!"
They jump into my arms for a cuddle
They give me sloppy kisses
Proudly show me schoolwork each day

My husband greets me with wild flowers
They picked together on a daily hike.
He arranges them into unruly bunches
As colorful and complete as our new life.

Small tonight

I want to be small tonight
Safe like a baby
Curled in your lap
Cuddled in your arms

Lead me to your bed
My hand in your warm paw
Be my hairy beast
Love me hot and slow

Hold me long and close
Fit me tight
When we have arrived
We'll duet a lullaby

Bury your warm cheek
In my languid breasts
Dream my suckling baby
We'll both be small tonight.

I'm Glad Cats Don't Bark

Phoenix the Siamese
with searching blue eyes
accompanied the guests
making love on
the pullout sofa

Curious at the motion and sound
He clawed and scratched
around their heads, under the springs
leaping softly to the floor and back
squeezing into crevices
between the armrest and mattress
pouncing on their feet and the
undulating quilt

I'm glad cats don't bark
the man whispered while
only feet away their son
snored inside a sleeping bag.

The woman stifled a laugh
reached out to stroke sleek fur
causing skittish Phoenix
to slide away under her fingers
and continue its leaping,
scratching, watching

Pausing only at the
moment of release
to share in discreet
silent purring.

Water Buffalo

Draught…

The buffalo licks dry stones

On the riverbed

With Apologies to My Legs

My legs   are fat

Balloon calves   slim   ankles

I hide   them   inside   long

Pants   long   skirts   prop

Them   on   high   heels

I feign   fashion   dignity   style

To keep   my   secret   until

This   hot   sweaty   summer

Got me   to think   how   I miss

Cool   breezes   how   I long

For   that   red-dot   dress

Still   patient   in my   closet

Too chic   to discard
Too short   to wear

My legs are loyal   nimble and strong

Never any trouble till now the pain in one hip may mean a new joint
a new doctor or a new attitude
to love them now - flaunt them in nylons - wrap them around my
lover - cool them in summer breezes

While they still carry me.

11543681R00040

Made in the USA
Charleston, SC
04 March 2012